FOLLOW US ON
INSTAGRAM
@KindergartenEducation

THIS NOTEBOOK BELONGS TO:

MORE BOOKS BY SMART KIDS NOTEBOOKS
(SCAN THE QR CODE OR VISIT: bit.ly/smartkidsnotebooks)

LET'S BEGIN BY RECAPPING THE LETTERS OF THE ALPHABET

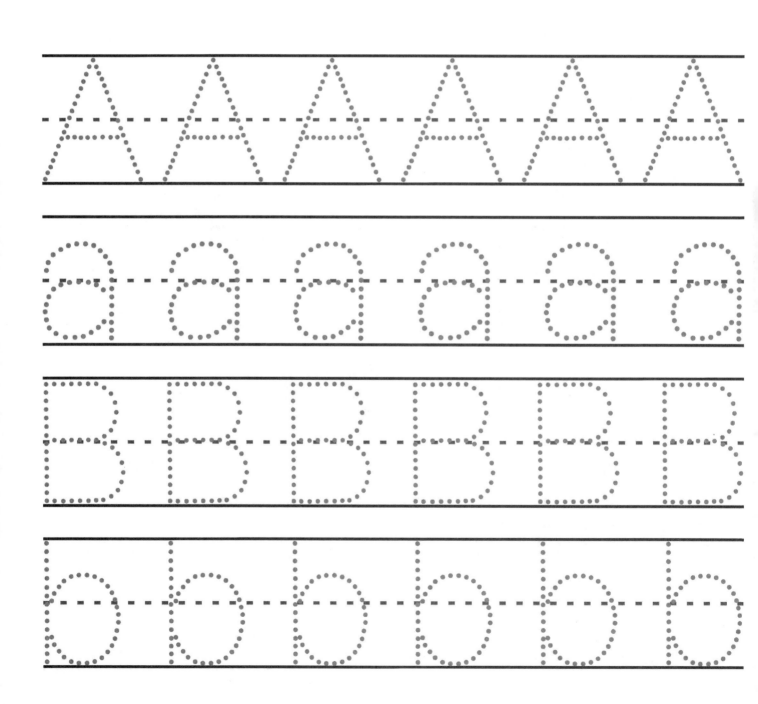

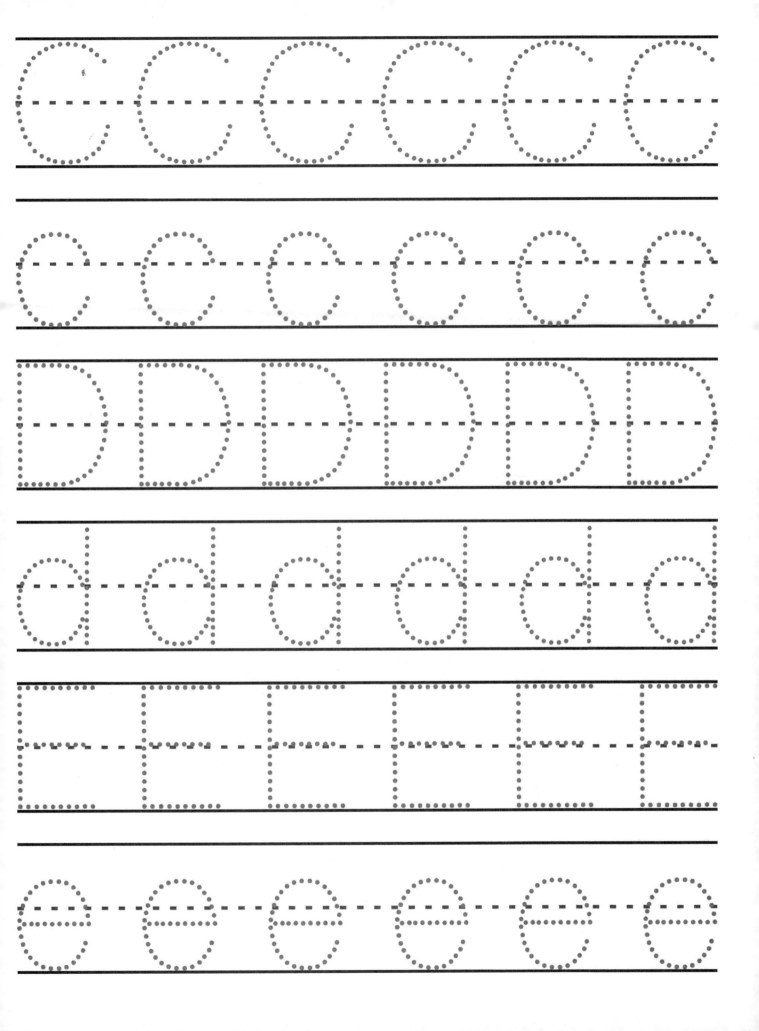

F F F F F F

f f f f f f

G G G G G G

g g g g g g

H H H H H H

h h h h h h

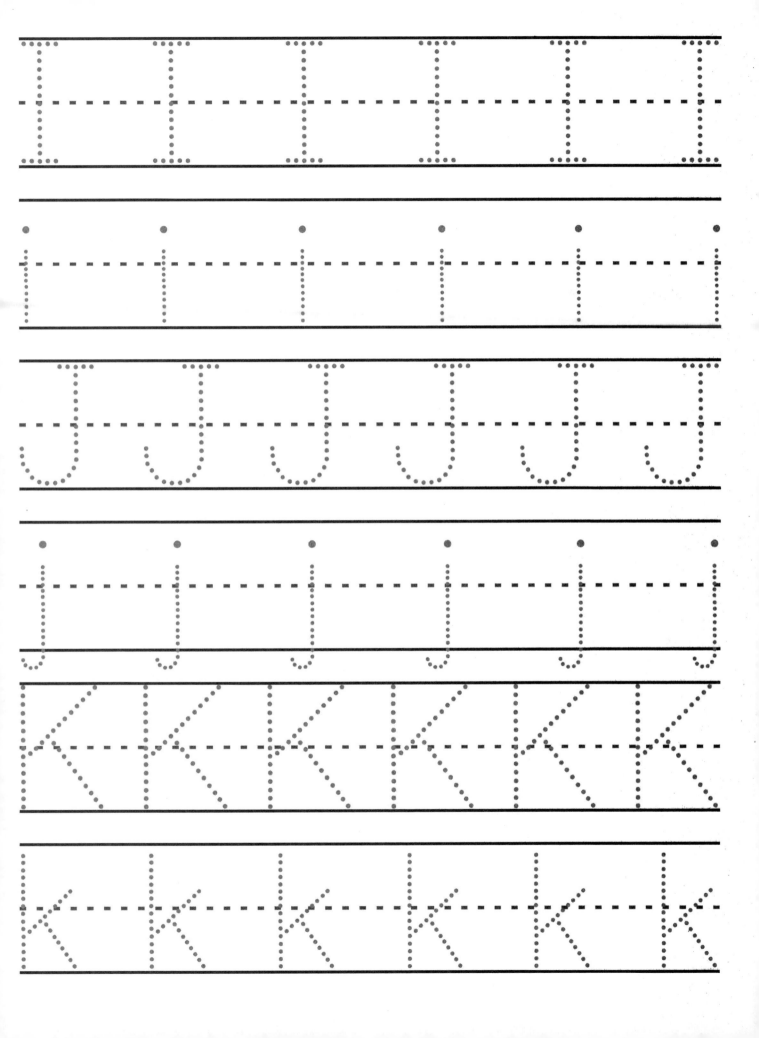

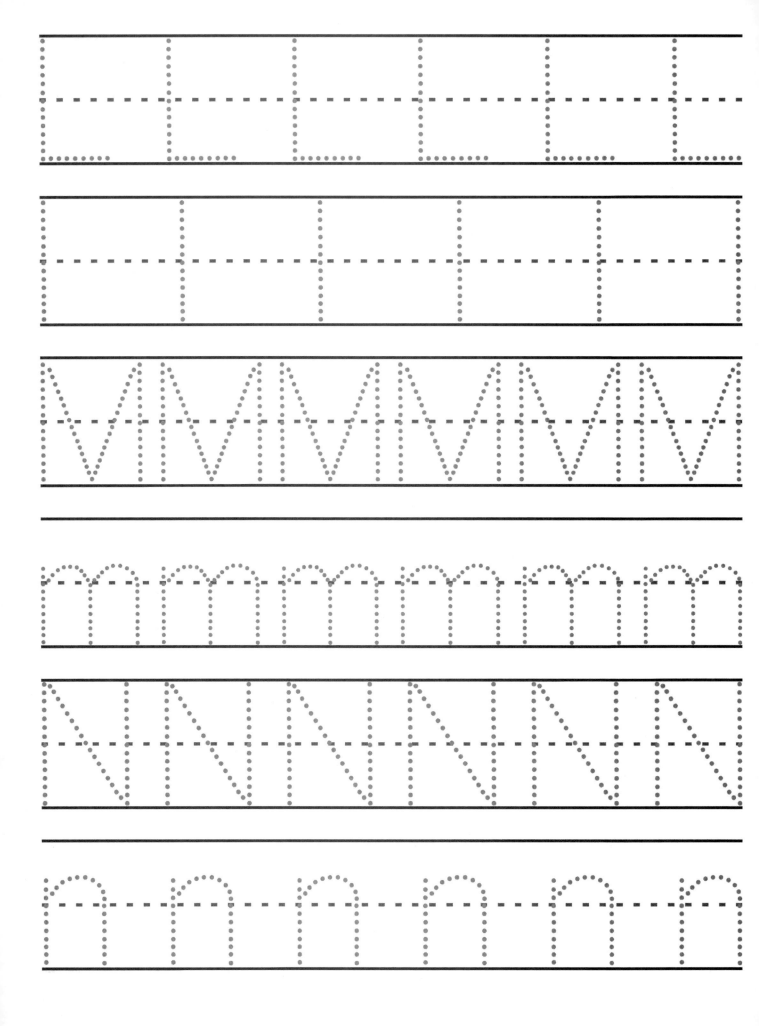

O O O O O O

O O O O O O

P P P P P P

b b b b b b

a a a a a a

a a a a a a

R R R R R R R

r r r r r r

S S S S S S

S S S S S S

I I I I I I

t t t t t t

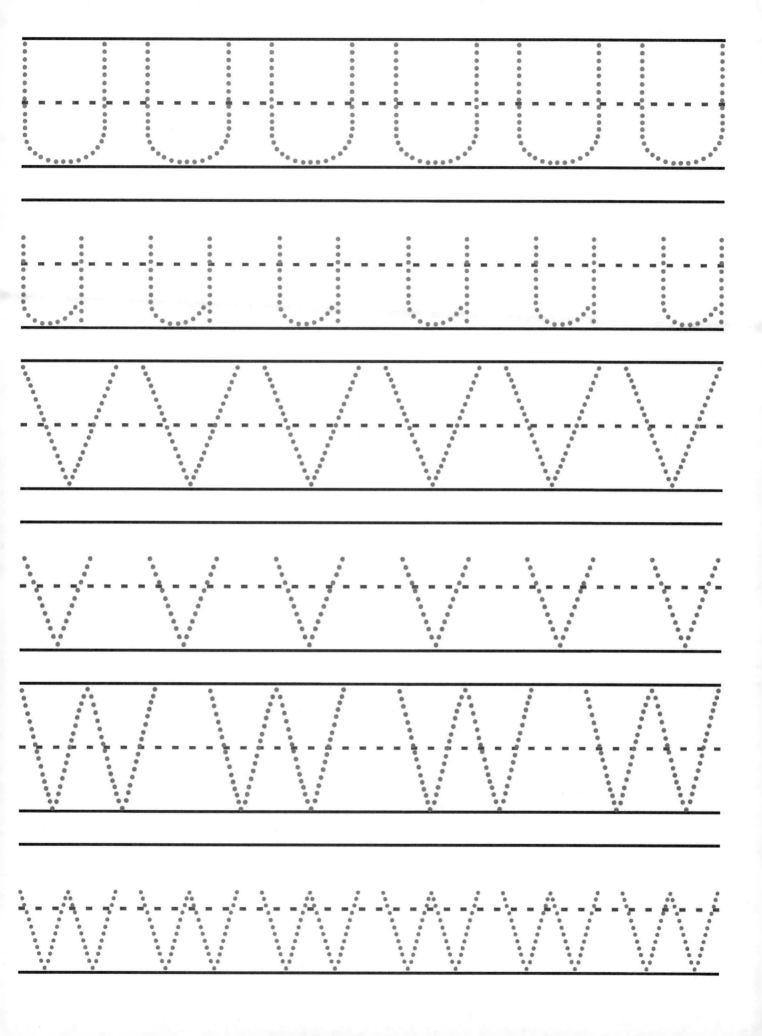

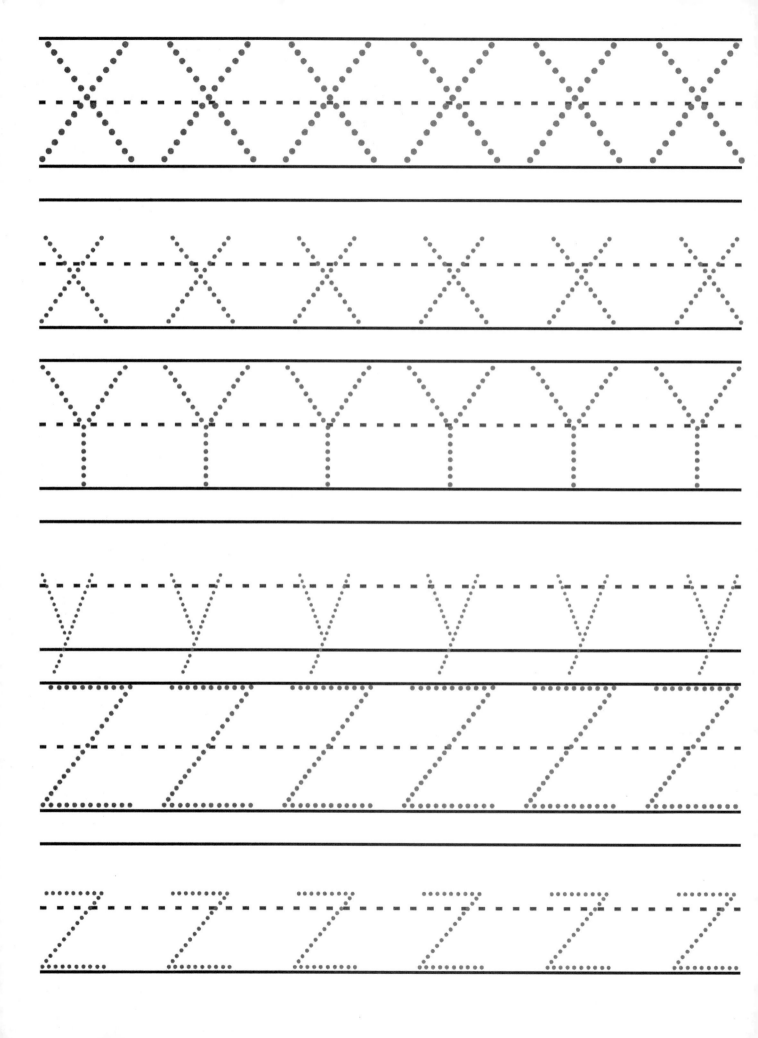

a

a a a a a a a a a

I saw __ bear.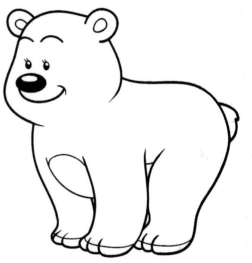

I saw a bear

and

and and and and

Mother _____ baby penguin.

Mother and baby penguin

away

away away away

Keep _____ from the snake.

Keep away from the snake

big

big   big   big   big

Elephants are ____.

Elephants are big

blue

blue blue blue blue

The _____ whale is the biggest animal.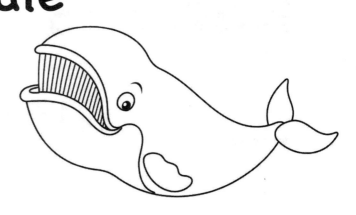

The blue whale is the biggest animal

can

can can can can

Rabbits

_____ jump.

Rabbits can jump

come

come come come

Lions _____
from Africa.

Lions come from Africa

down

down down down

The monkey
fell _____.

The monkey fell down

find

find find find find

I can't _____
my iguana.

I can't find my iguana

for

for for for for for

The ball is

_____ my cat.

The ball is for my cat

funny

funny funny funny

The monkey is _____.

The monkey is funny

go

go go go go go go

Storks ____ south in the winter.

Storks go south

help

help   help   help

Dolphins

_____ humans.

Dolphins help humans

here

here   here   here

Buffalos live

_____.

Buffalos live here

I

I I I I I I

___ am tall.

I am tall I am tall

in

in   in   in   in   in   in

Rhinos live
___ Africa.

Rhinos live in Africa

is

is   is   is   is   is   is

The elephant ___ big.

The elephant is big

it

it it it it it it

_____ is prickly.

It is prickly

jump

jump   jump   jump

Kangaroos can

_____.

Kangaroos can jump

little

little   little   little

The ant is

_____.

The ant is little

look

look   look   look

Crocodiles

_____ scary.

Crocodiles look scary

make

make make make

Birds _____ nests.

Birds make nests

me

me me me me me

Unicorns make
___ happy.

Unicons make me happy

my

my my my my my

Dogs are
____ friends.

Dogs are my friends

not

not not not not

Mice are

_____ big.

Mice are not big

one

one one one one

We have

_____ cow.

We have one cow

play

play   play   play

Hippos like to _____.

Hippos like to play

red

red red red red

Ladybugs are _____.

Ladybugs are red

run

run run run run

Cheetahs can
_____ fast.

Cheetahs can run fast

said

said said said said

The parrot
_____ a joke.

The parrot said a joke

see

see see see see

Owls can _____ at night.

Owls can see at night

the

the the the the

I saw ____
zebra.

I saw the zebra

three

three three three

I see _____ fish.

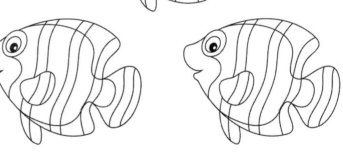

I see three fish

to

to to to to to to to

The bee came
___ me.

The bee came to me

two

two two two two

I see _____ frogs.

I see two frogs

up

up   up   up   up   up

Birds fly ___ in the sky.

Birds fly up in the sky

we

we   we   we   we

____ saw a
jellyfish
on the beach

We saw a jellyfish

where

where   where

_____ is my turtle?

Where is my turtle

yellow

yellow   yellow

Baby chickens are _____.

Baby chickens are yellow

you

you you you you

Did _____ see
the deer?

Did you see the deer

all

all all all all all

I love ___
camels.

I love all camels

am

am   am   am   am

I ____ a
good friend.

I am a good friend

are

are are are are

There ____
many bees.

There are many bees

at

at at at at at at at

I looked ___
the emu.

I looked at the emu

ate

ate ate ate ate

The bear ____ the honey.

The bear ate the honey

be

be be be be be

The fox will ___ back.

The fox will be back

black

black black black

The cat is

_____.

The cat is black

brown

brown brown brown

The deer is

_____.

The deer is brown

but

but but but but

_____ I don't like snakes.

But I don't like snakes

came

came came came

The ferret _____ to us.

The ferret came to us

did

did did did did

_____ you see the frog?

Did you see the frog

do

do do do do do

____ you like penguins?

Do you like penguins

eat

eat eat eat eat

Cows ____ grass.

Cows eat grass

four

four   four   four

We have _____ rabbits.

We have four rabbits

get

get get get get

Whales

_____ very big.

Whales get very big

good

good good good

Parrots are
_____ pets.

Parrots are good pets

have

have have have

Iguanas _____ tails.

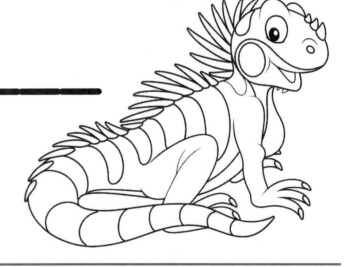

Iguanas have tails

he

he he he he he

___ likes horses.

He likes horses

into

into into into into

Don't bring ants
_____ my house.

Don't bring ants into

| like |

like like like like

I _____
birds.

I like birds

must

must must must

Hippos

_____

eat a lot.

Hippos must eat a lot

new

new new new

She got a
_____ fish.

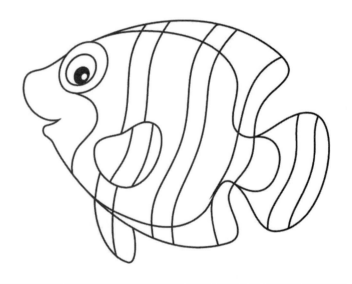

She got a new fish

no

no no no no no

_____ pets are
allowed here.

No pets are allowed

now

now now now

_____ we have a goat.

Now we have a goat

on

on on on on on

We saw a
koala ___
the tree.

We saw a koala on the tree

our

our our our our

We saw a
racoon in ___
backyard.

We saw a racoon in

our backyard

out

out out out out

A camel escaped ___ of the zoo.

A camel escaped out of the zoo

please

please please

Can I _____ go to the zoo?

Can I please go to the zoo

pretty

pretty   pretty

Swans are

_____.

Swans are pretty

ran

ran ran ran ran

My mouse
_____ away.

My mouse ran away

ride

ride   ride   ride

I can _____
a horse.

I can ride a horse

saw

saw   saw   saw

I _____

a hedgehog.

I saw a hedgehog

say

say say say say

Parrots can _____ words.

Parrots can say words

she

she she she she

_____ likes giraffes.

She likes giraffes

SO

So So So So So So

Ants are
____ small.

Ants are so small

soon

soon soon soon

We will go to
Australia _____.

We will go to
Australia soon

that

that that that

_____ is an

elephant.

That is an elephant

there

there   there

_____ is a
yak in the zoo.

There is a yak in the zoo

they

they they they

_____ saw

a vulture.

They saw a vulture

this

this   this   this

_____ is a

x-ray fish.

This is a x-ray fish

too

too too too too

I like rhinos

_____.

I like rhinos too

under

under   under

Fish live _____

water.

Fish live under water

want

want want want

I _____ a dog.

I want a dog

was

was was was was

The bear

_____ hungry.

The bear was hungry

well

well well well well

Seals can
swim _____.

Seals can swim well

went

went went went

The cat _____
to the doctor.

The cat went to the doctor

what

what what what

_____ is the bird doing here?

What is the bird doing here

white

white white white

_____ bears
can swim.

White bears can swim

who

who who who who

_____ likes turtles?

Who likes turtles

will

will will will will

I _____ grow big.

I will grow big

with

with   with   with

Playing _____
pets is fun.

Playing with pets is fun

yes

yes yes yes yes

_____, I like unicorns.

Yes, I like unicorns

an

an an an an an an

I saw ____
owl on the tree.

I saw an owl on the tree

any

any any any any

I didn't see
_____ whales.

I didn't see any whales

fly

fly   fly   fly   fly

Bees can _____  very fast.

Bees can fly very fast

from

from   from   from

Hippos are
_____
Africa.

Hippos are from Africa

has

has has has has

The deer
_____ horns.

The deer has horns

live

live live live live

Parrots _____ long.

Parrots live long

some

some some some

_____ birds

are big.

Some birds are big

walk

walk walk walk

Turtles _____ slowly.

Turtles walk slowly